To...

From...

Date...

Whoever is happy will make
others happy, too.

MARK TWAIN

This Little ♡ Light of Mine

seeker of all things true

artwork by Kelly Rae Roberts
written by Hope Lyda

H™
HARVEST HOUSE PUBLISHERS
EUGENE, OREGON

This Little Light of Mine

Artwork copyright © by Kelly Rae Roberts
Text copyright © 2013 by Harvest House Publishers. Original text by
Hope Lyda.

Published by Harvest House Publishers
Eugene, Oregon 97402
www.harvesthousepublishers.com

ISBN 978-0-7369-5061-9

The artwork of Kelly Rae Roberts is used by Harvest House Publishers, Inc.,
under authorization from Courtney Davis, Inc. For more information regard-
ing art prints featured in this book, please contact:

Courtney Davis, Inc.
55 Francisco Street, Suite 450
San Francisco, CA 94133
www.courtneydavis.com

Design and production by Dugan Design Group, Bloomington, Minnesota

Harvest House Publishers has made every effort to trace the ownership of
all poems and quotes. In the event of a question arising from the use of a
poem or quote, we regret any error made and will be pleased to make the
necessary correction in future editions of this book.

All Scripture quotations are taken from the *Holy Bible*, New Living
Translation, copyright © 1996, 2004. Used by permission of Tyndale House
Publishers, Inc., Wheaton, IL 60189 USA. All rights reserved.

Printed in China

13 14 15 16 17 18 19 / LP / 10 9 8 7 6 5 4 3 2 1

Someday perhaps the inner light will shine forth from us,
and then we'll need no other light.

JOHANN WOLFGANG VON GOETHE

surrender
your
fear

Contents

Life must be lived as play. PLATO

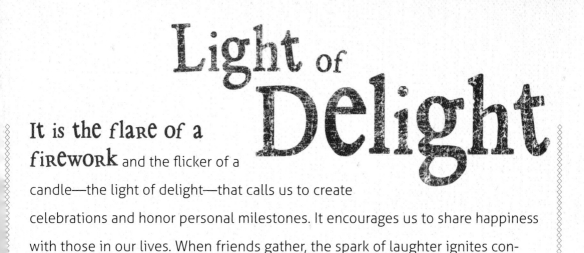

Light of Delight

It is the flare of a firework and the flicker of a candle—the light of delight—that calls us to create celebrations and honor personal milestones. It encourages us to share happiness with those in our lives. When friends gather, the spark of laughter ignites connection between kindred spirits. And we gasp in awe at how joy replenishes joy.

Our brightest blazes of gladness are commonly kindled by unexpected sparks.
Samuel Johnson

Happiness is a sunbeam which may pass through a thousand bosoms without losing a particle of its original ray; nay, when it strikes on a kindred heart, like the converged light on a mirror, it reflects itself with redoubled brightness. It is not perfected till it is shared.

JANE PORTER

For everything that lives is holy,
life delights in life.

WILLIAM BLAKE

Her loveliness I never knew
Until she smiled on me:
Oh! then I saw her eye was bright,
a well of love, a spring of light.

HARTLEY COLERIDGE

all beings live from light; each fair created thing, the very plants, turn with a joyful transport to the light.

JOHANN CHRISTOPH FRIEDRICH VON SCHILLER

the
beauty of life lives
inside the smallest
of moments
(pay attention)

Creating is
the true essence
of life.

BARTHOLD GEORG NIEBUHR

He that has light within his
own clear breast
May sit i' th' centre and
enjoy bright day.

JOHN MILTON

seeker of all things true

9

Dear Hope,

Thank you for your unending LIGHT, your truth, and for making my heart flutter.

soar

Light of Hope

When we need to find the next step, hope shows us the way. Lanterns lit with the promise of something good are placed by caring hands at each bend in the road. If a shadow falls upon the trail, we need never feel alone. We are accompanied by hope and her companion, love. Set out with these friends and witness the beauty of the unfolding mystery.

Hope is like the sun, which, as we journey toward it, casts the shadow of our burden behind us.

SAMUEL SMILES

Walk boldly and wisely in the light thou hast; there is a hand above will help thee on.

PHILLIP JAMES BAILEY

Hope, like the gleaming taper's light,
adorns and cheers our way.

OLIVER GOLDSMITH

There is no medicine like hope, no incentive so
great, and no tonic so powerful as expectation of
something better to-morrow.

ORISON SWETT MARDEN

Hope is the only bee that makes honey
without flowers.

ROBERT INGERSOLL

you
are a gift to this world

When one door closes,
another opens;
but we often look so long
and so regretfully
upon the closed door that
we do not see the one
which has opened for us.

ALEXANDER GRAHAM BELL

hope

Light of Possibility

Let there be light!

Creation began with the possibility of an impossibility. Our hearts, minds, and souls are eager to join in the passionate act of dreaming something breath-taking into being. This imagination and potential was entrusted to us so that we might scatter vibrant hues across the canvas of each day and share a vision of "what could be" with others.

> Our aspirations
> are our possibilities.
>
> SAMUEL JOHNSON

> Man is so made that
> when anything fires his soul,
> impossibilities vanish.
>
> JEAN DE LA FONTAINE

On the imagination God sometimes
paints, by dream and symbol, the
likeness of things to come.

EDWARD BULWER-LYTTON

Far away there in the sunshine are
my highest aspirations. I may not
reach them, but I can look up and see
their beauty, believe in them, and
try to follow where they lead.

LOUISA MAY ALCOTT

There is radiance and glory in the
darkness could we but see—and to see
we have only to look.

FRA GIOVANNI GIOCONDO

GOD dreamed—the suns sprang flaming
into place, and sailing worlds with many a
venturous race. He woke—His smile
alone illumined space.

AMBROSE BIERCE

believe
in
possibility

a man should learn to detect
and watch that gleam of light which
flashes across his mind from within.
RALPH WALDO EMERSON

What is now proved, was
once only imagined.
WILLIAM BLAKE

Hope is the dream of a soul awake. FRENCH PROVERB

Wish

(dream)

(imagine)

xo

Seize this very minute!
What you can do, or dream
you can, begin it;
Boldness has genius, power
and magic in it.

JOHANN WOLFGANG VON GOETHE

what
sets
your
heart
Free ?

surrender

Light of Faith

The beacon of faith illuminates our souls and fills the corners of our hearts where doubt might want to reside. It embraces us when we are stubborn or scared. The good news is that we cannot outdo or use up faith because it comes from an endless source. Each morning our hope can rise with the sun because we know the wonder of wishes and the tender kiss of a love everlasting.

There they stand, the innumerable stars, shining n order like a living hymn, written in light.

NATHANIEL PARKER WILLIS

Every great enterprise begins with and takes its first forward step in faith.

AUGUST WILHELM VON SCHLEGEL

The windows of my soul I throw
Wide open to the sun.

JOHN GREENLEAF WHITTIER

Grace comes into the soul, as the
morning sun into the world; first a
dawning; then a light; and at last the sun
in his full and excellent brightness.

THOMAS ADAMS

In dreams
and in love
there are no
impossibilities.

JANOS ARANY

God is light.

THE BOOK OF FIRST JOHN

Live in rooms full of light.

AULUS CORNELIUS CELSUS

To see a world in a grain of sand
and a Heaven in a wild flower,
Hold Infinity in the palm of your
hand and eternity in an hour.

WILLIAM BLAKE

what
Makes your
heart
flutter

Light of Love

Love is kindled in the hearth of the heart. It comforts, stirs, and sparks. Like any source of light, when love is lifted high, more people are able to see by it, move forward in it, and experience its warmth. The affection and adoration you give and receive makes you sparkle more brilliantly and soar a little higher.

We are shaped and fashioned by what we love.

JOHANN WOLFGANG VON GOETHE

Love is an image of God, and not a lifeless image, but the living essence of the divine nature which beams full of all goodness.

MARTIN LUTHER

Write your name in kindness, love, and mercy on the hearts of the thousands you come in contact with, year by year, and you will never be forgotten. Your name, your deeds, will be as legible on the hearts you leave behind, as the stars on the brow of evening.

THOMAS CHALMERS

Happiness is not perfected until it is shared.

JANE PORTER

The place to be happy is here.
The time to be happy is now.
The way to be happy
is to make others so.

ROBERT INGERSOLL

Through love to light! Oh wonderful the way
That leads from darkness to the perfect day!

RICHARD WATSON GILDER

whene'er yo
our beauty
he air with fr
simple breath.

what if you let love HEAL your heart?

Love gives itself; it is not bought. HENRY WADSWORTH LONGFELLOW

beloved win

just

fo

he

To love and to be loved is the greatest happiness of existence.

SYDNEY SMITH

There is in life no blessing like affection; it soothes, it hallows, elevates, subdues, and bringeth down to earth its native heaven.

LETITIA ELIZABETH LANDON

The conversation of a friend brightens the eyes.

PERSIAN PROVERB

Light of Courage

It's a fabulous adventure to discover our paths to purpose. Every leap of faith, starting line, dream, daring pursuit, and detour awakens our recognition of the person we are each intended to become. The moment it dawns on us that nobody else in the world can step up to be us...we are empowered to shine bravely and brightly all the days of our lives.

I try to avoid looking forward or backward, and try to keep looking upward.

CHARLOTTE BRONTË

Go on with a spirit that fears nothing!

HOMER

Do not anticipate trouble,
or worry about what may never happen.
Keep in the sunlight.

BENJAMIN FRANKLIN

Bravery never goes out of fashion.

WILLIAM MAKEPEACE THACKERAY

To be yourself, simple, honest, and
unpretending, you will enjoy through life
the respect and love of friends.

WILLIAM SHERMAN

Light is the symbol of truth.

JAMES RUSSELL LOWELL

Though my soul may set in darkness,
it will rise in perfect light;
I have loved the stars too fondly
to be fearful of the night.

SARAH WILLIAMS

your story matters

(tell it

hap'pily
lov'ed.

Be not afraid of life.
Believe that life is worth
living and your belief
will help create the fact.

WILLIAM JAMES

There are two ways of
spreading light:
to be the candle or the
mirror that reflects it.

EDITH WHARTON

Light of Gratitude

As children we'd lie down in the grass, close our eyes, and lift our faces to the sun. What a gift it was to have shimmering rays flit and flash across our cheeks. Oh, how we still need to give ourselves over to such goodness. Let's fall back into the lushness of a savored life and watch beams of blessing and glimmers of gratitude parade across our minds. Only when we are thankful do we notice the many colorful pieces that make up our personal, exquisite kaleidoscope.

A grateful mind is both a great and a happy mind.

WILLIAM SECKER

Live in rooms full of light.

AULUS CORNELIUS CELSUS

It is not how much we have,
but how much we enjoy,
that makes happiness.

CHARLES SPURGEON

Hope is the best part of our riches.

CHRISTIAN NESTELL BOVEE

Contentment opens the
source of every joy.

JAMES BEATTIE

Seas roll to waft me,
suns to light me rise;
My footstool earth,
my canopy the skies.

ALEXANDER POPE

Light tomorrow
with today.

ELIZABETH BARRETT BROWNING

blessec

Let the thankful heart
sweep through the day and, as the magnet finds the iron,
so it will find, in every hour, some heavenly blessings!

HENRY WARD BEECHER

Let us be grateful to
people who make us happy,
they are the charming
gardeners who make our
souls blossom.

MARCEL PROUST

How blessings
brighten as
they take their
flight!

EDWARD YOUNG

The sunshine of life is
made up of very little
beams that are bright
all the time.

JOHN AIKIN

Light of Kindness

Whether it is a comforting word, a sincere offer of help, or an invitation to laugh and cry with gusto, kindness is a jewel we share with another. We hold it up to the light and ooh and ahh over its capacity to illume the space between friends and strangers. When we gently blow on the whisper white of a dandelion and make a big, delicious wish, let it be that the golden rule glows in all that we do and in all that we are.

a laugh, to be *joyous*, must flow from a *joyous* heart, for without kindness there can be no true joy.

THOMAS CARLYLE

a good deed is never lost. He who
sows courtesy reaps friendship,
and he who plants kindness
gathers love.

SAINT BASIL

How rare and wonderful is
that flash of a moment
when we realize we have
discovered a friend.

WILLIAM E. ROTHSCHILD

Kind hearts are the gardens;
Kind thoughts are the roots;
Kind words are the flowers;
Kind deeds are the fruits.
Take care of the gardens
and keep out the weeds.
Fill it with sunshine,
Kind words and kind deeds.

HENRY WADSWORTH LONGFELLOW

noblest things, which are sweetness and light.

JONATHAN SWIFT

together
our
hearts
were
wide

Friendship is precious, not only in the
shade, but in the sunshine of life, and thanks to
a benevolent arrangement of things, the greater
part of life is sunshine.

THOMAS JEFFERSON

All God's pleasures are simple ones; health,
the rapture of a May morning, sunshine, the stream
blue and green, kind words, benevolent acts, the glow
of good humor.

FREDERICK WILLIAM ROBERTSON

As gold more splendid from the first appears;
Thus friendship brightens by the length of years.

THOMAS CARLYLE

Happiness is a perfume you can't pour on others
without getting a few drops on yourself.

RALPH WALDO EMERSON

a kind word will give more pleasure than a present.

SIR JOHN LUBBOCK

Even a small star shines in the darkness.

FINNISH PROVERB

Do all the good you can, in all the ways you can, to all the souls you can, in every place you can, at all the times you can, with all the zeal you can, as long as ever you can.

JOHN WESLEY